Enslow
PUBLISHING

INVESTIGATE!

WHO'S THE GREATEST? Sports Stars

CONNOR MCDAVID VS. WAYNE GRETZKY

KATHLEEN CONNORS

HOCKEY'S GREATEST

Please visit our website, www.enslow.com. For a free color catalog of all our high-quality books, call toll free 1-800-398-2504 or fax 1-877-980-4454.

Library of Congress Cataloging-in-Publication Data

Names: Connors, Kathleen author
Title: Connor McDavid vs. Wayne Gretzky : hockey's greatest / Kathleen Connors.
Other titles: Connor McDavid versus Wayne Gretzky
Description: Buffalo, New York : Enslow Publishing, 2026. | Series: Who's the greatest?. Sports stars | Includes index.
Identifiers: LCCN 2025030205 (print) | LCCN 2025030206 (ebook) | ISBN 9781978546936 library binding | ISBN 9781978546929 paperback | ISBN 9781978546943 ebook
Subjects: LCSH: McDavid, Connor, 1997—Juvenile literature | Gretzky, Wayne, 1961—Juvenile literature | Hockey players–Canada–Biography–Juvenile literature | LCGFT: Biographies
Classification: LCC GV848.5.M395 C66 2026 (print) | LCC GV848.5.M395 (ebook) | DDC 796.962092–dc23/eng/20250923
LC record available at https://lccn.loc.gov/2025030205
LC ebook record available at https://lccn.loc.gov/2025030206

Published in 2026 by
Enslow Publishing
2544 Clinton Street
Buffalo, NY 14224

Designer: Tanya Dellaccio Keeney
Editor: Kristen Rajzak Nelson and Therese Shea

Photo credits: Cover (McDavid) JASON FRANSON/AP Images; cover (Gretzky) STF/AP Images; pp. 5 (Gretzky), 10 Francis Specker/Alamy Images; pp. 5 (McDavid), 9, 15, 19, 22, 23, 25 ZUMA Press, Inc./Alamy Images; p. 7 roger tillberg/Alamy Images; pp. 11, 17, 27 Gints Ivuskans/Shutterstock.com; p. 12 Richard Bartlaga/Flickr.com; p. 13 https://upload.wikimedia.org/wikipedia/commons/3/36/Connor_McDavid_07042015.jpg; p. 14 CelebrityArchaeology.com/Aamy Images; p. 16 PA Images/Alamy Images; p. 21 https://upload.wikimedia.org/wikipedia/commons/7/74/Connor_McDavid_of_the_Edmonton_Oilers_%28cropped%29.jpg; p. 24 Paul McKinnon/Shutterstock.com; p. 26 https://upload.wikimedia.org/wikipedia/commons/c/cb/Hart_Memorial_Trophy_%2848667773012%29.jpg; p. 29 (McDavid) SOPA Images Limited/Alamy Images; p. 29 (Gretzky) Debby Wong/Shutterstock.com.

Printed in the United States of America

CPSIA compliance information: Batch #CW26ENS: For further information contact Enslow Publishing, at 1-800-398-2504.

CONTENTS

Words in the glossary appear in **bold** type the first time they are used in the text.

HOCKEY GREATNESS

Wayne Gretzky is known to hockey fans as simply "The Great One." He's widely considered the GOAT—greatest of all time. In fact, when Gretzky **retired** in 1999, he held 61 National Hockey League (NHL) records. Some of these are unlikely to ever be broken.

However, Connor McDavid has been called the best hockey player of his **generation**. He continues to wow fans on the ice as a member of the Edmonton Oilers today.

Did You Know?

McDavid plays center. So did Gretzky!

WAYNE GRETZKY

CONNOR MCDAVID

MCDAVID IS A MODERN SUPERSTAR WHO HAS BEEN COMPARED TO GRETZKY MANY TIMES. SOME OF THAT COMPARISON IS BECAUSE BOTH GRETZKY AND MCDAVID PLAYED FOR THE OILERS!

GET TO KNOW GRETZKY

Wayne Gretzky was born on January 26, 1961, in Ontario, Canada. His parents, Walter and Phyllis, lived in the city of Brantford starting shortly after Gretzky was born. Gretzky was the oldest of five children. He has a younger sister and three younger brothers.

Gretzky learned to ice-skate around age two. Later, his dad built an ice rink in the family's backyard. Here, Gretzky learned to play hockey. He got to be so good, he played in a **league** with 10-year-olds at age 6!

Did You Know?

Hockey is one of Canada's national sports.

WALTER GRETZKY FLOODED THE FAMILY'S BACKYARD TO MAKE AN ICE RINK SO HIS SON COULD SKATE AS LONG AS HE WANTED—AND WALTER WOULDN'T HAVE TO WAIT FOR HIM IN THE COLD!

MEET MCDAVID

Connor McDavid was born on January 13, 1997. His family lived in Richmond Hill, Ontario, north of the big city of Toronto, Canada. McDavid and his older brother Cameron first learned to ski and then ice-skate. McDavid started playing hockey around age three—even though kids were supposed to be five years old to start in the league!

As a child, McDavid became known as a hockey prodigy. Into his teens, he was always playing with kids who were older than him.

Did You Know?

A prodigy is a child or young person who is especially talented in a sport or other activity.

MCDAVID WAS A FAN OF THE TORONTO MAPLE LEAFS NHL TEAM WHEN HE WAS GROWING UP.

JUNIORS HOCKEY

As a teenager, Gretzky kept moving to more **competitive** leagues. During the 1977–1978 season, Gretzky was second in scoring for the whole Ontario Hockey Association. In 1978, he played for Canada in the World Junior Championship. He led the **tournament** in scoring!

ROOKIE OF THE YEAR, TORONTO METRO JUNIOR B LEAGUE, 1975–1976

TOP CENTER, HIGH SCORER, WORLD JUNIOR CHAMPIONSHIP, 1978

GRETZKY WAS ONE OF THE BEST PLAYERS —IF NOT THE BEST PLAYER— ON EVERY TEAM HE PLAYED ON AS A CHILD AND TEENAGER.

Did You Know?

Around 1977, Gretzky started wearing number 99. His usual number 9 was taken on the team at that time.

McDavid was so good, he was allowed to play on a **major junior** team at age 15, a year early. In addition, he won a gold medal as part of Team Canada at the World Under-18 Championship held in Russia.

MCDAVID PLAYED FOR HIS COUNTRY AS PART OF TEAM CANADA WHEN HE WAS STILL A TEENAGER.

TOP SCORER IN UNDER-18 WORLD CHAMPIONSHIP TOURNAMENT, 2013

GOLD MEDALIST, WORLD JUNIOR CHAMPIONSHIP, 2015

GOLD MEDALIST, MVP, TOP FORWARD IN UNDER-18 WORLD CHAMPIONSHIP, 2013

DRAFTED—OR NOT

Gretzky wasn't **drafted** into the NHL. When he was just 17, he started playing for the Indianapolis Racers, a **professional** team that was part of the World Hockey Association (WHA). He didn't play on the team long. The Edmonton Oilers bought his contract in 1978.

GRETZKY STAYED WITH EDMONTON THE FOLLOWING YEAR WHEN THE OILERS WERE ONE OF THE WHA TEAMS TO JOIN THE NHL.

SIGNED 21-YEAR CONTRACT WITH THE OILERS AT AGE 18

Did You Know?

At the time Gretzky started playing professional hockey, players had to be at least 20 years old to be drafted into the NHL.

McDavid played three years in the Ontario Hockey League (OHL). Then, at age 18, he was drafted first in the 2015 NHL Draft by the Edmonton Oilers. At the time, McDavid said it was a "dream come true."

WHEN MCDAVID WAS DRAFTED, PLAYERS WHO TURNED 18 BEFORE SEPTEMBER 15 OF THE DRAFT YEAR COULD BE DRAFTED. THIS IS STILL THE RULE TODAY.

NUMBER ONE NHL DRAFT PICK, 2015

Did You Know?

The OHL is one of the major junior hockey leagues that make up the Canadian Hockey League. Players are commonly between the ages of 16 and 20.

EARLY SUCCESS

Gretzky immediately made an impact on the Oilers. He scored 51 goals and had 86 assists in his first season. The following season, he averaged more than two points a game. No one else in NHL history had ever done that!

SET THE REGULAR-SEASON NHL RECORD FOR GOALS, ASSISTS, AND TOTAL POINTS, 1981–1982*

*HE BROKE HIS OWN RECORDS FOR ASSISTS AND TOTAL POINTS IN THE 1985–1986 SEASON.

GRETZKY STARTED SETTING RECORDS EARLY IN HIS NHL CAREER.

McDavid only played 45 games in his first NHL season. However, in his second season (2016–2017), he was named captain of the Oilers. He led the league in scoring that season and took the Oilers to the playoffs for the first time in many years.

YOUNGEST TEAM CAPTAIN IN NHL HISTORY (19 YEARS, 266 DAYS OLD)

TED LINDSAY AWARD (PLAYER'S CHOICE OF MOST OUTSTANDING PLAYER), 2017

MCDAVID MADE UP FOR HIS SHORT ROOKIE, OR FIRST, SEASON BY BECOMING A SUPERSTAR FOR THE OILERS IN HIS SECOND SEASON.

Did You Know?

McDavid sat out 37 games of the 2015–2016 season with an injury.

INTERNATIONAL PLAY

The 1998 Winter Olympics was the first time players from the NHL took part in the Olympics. Gretzky played for Team Canada. The team seemed to be full of superstars but lost in a shootout against the Czech team and came in fourth.

ONE-TIME OLYMPIAN

EVEN THOUGH HE WAS ONE OF THE TOP SCORERS IN THE NHL, GRETZKY WASN'T CHOSEN TO TAKE PART IN THE SHOOTOUT AT THE 1998 OLYMPICS.

McDavid hasn't played in the Olympics, though it's likely he will in 2026. In 2025, McDavid was on Team Canada at the 4 Nations Face-Off Tournament. The United States, Finland, and Sweden also took part. Team Canada won!

THOUGH HE ISN'T AN OLYMPIAN YET, MCDAVID HAS PLAYED FOR TEAM CANADA AT THE WORLD CHAMPIONSHIPS.

Did You Know?

McDavid scored the winning goal in the final game of the 4 Nations Face-Off Tournament.

GRETZKY'S RECORDS

At the end of Gretzky's career, he held the record for the most points of any NHL player ever. He also had the record for the most goals! His goal-scoring record stood until 2025, when Alex Ovechkin broke it.

Gretzky also holds the record for the most assists by a player in NHL history, as well as most assists by a player in one season. He still holds the record for most goals in a single season too.

Did You Know?

As of mid-2025, Gretzky holds the record number of career points for the Oilers.

2,857 CAREER POINTS

894 CAREER GOALS

1,963 CAREER ASSISTS

163 ASSISTS IN ONE SEASON

92 GOALS IN ONE SEASON

GRETZKY'S ACCOMPLISHMENTS WERE HONORED IN THE HOCKEY WORLD WHEN THE NHL RETIRED HIS NUMBER 99.

MCDAVID MAKES HIS MARK

In his decade playing for the Oilers, McDavid has risen to second in the **franchise** with career points. Only the Great One himself is ahead of McDavid! McDavid has other impressive stats too.

He has had eight seasons of more than 100 points as of 2025, which is tied for the third most in NHL history. He was also the fourth-fastest player to reach 1,000 career points when he did so in his 659th NHL game.

Did You Know?

The Art Ross Trophy is given to the NHL player who has the most points at the end of each season. The Maurice Richard Trophy is given to the top-scoring player in the NHL. Gretzky holds the record for most Art Ross Trophies in a career with 10 wins.

CAREER-HIGH POINTS IN ONE SEASON: 153 (2022–2023)

99TH NHL PLAYER EVER TO REACH 1,000 CAREER POINTS

FIVE-TIME WINNER OF THE ART ROSS TROPHY

ONE-TIME WINNER OF THE MAURICE RICHARD TROPHY

SINCE MCDAVID IS STILL PLAYING IN THE NHL, SOME OF THESE STATS, GIVEN AS OF MID-2025, ARE LIKELY TO CHANGE.

ALL-STARS

Gretzky holds records in NHL All-Star Games too. He has the most career goals in All-Star Games as well as the most goals scored in one All-Star Game (4 in 1983). Gretzky has the most career points in All-Star Games and the most career assists too.

IN GRETZKY'S LAST ALL-STAR GAME IN 1999, HE WAS NAMED MVP, OR MOST VALUABLE PLAYER. HE WAS GIVEN A TRUCK AS A PRIZE!

18 NHL ALL-STAR GAMES

McDavid played in his first NHL All-Star Game in 2017. He was named to the event every year it was held after that. In 2024, he won $1 million for winning the skills competition that was held during that All-Star Weekend!

7 NHL ALL-STAR GAMES

THE NHL DIDN'T HOLD AN ALL-STAR GAME IN 2021 BECAUSE OF THE COVID-19 PANDEMIC. IT ALSO DIDN'T HOLD ONE IN 2025. INSTEAD, PLAYERS TOOK PART IN THE 4 NATIONS FACE-OFF TOURNAMENT, WHICH MCDAVID PLAYED IN.

Did You Know?

Over the years, how players are chosen for the NHL All-Star Game has changed a few times. Often, players are chosen for the NHL All-Star Game by those in charge at the NHL and a vote by fans.

THE STANLEY CUP

Gretzky led the Oilers to win the NHL championship for the first time during the 1983–1984 season. The team followed that Stanley Cup win with another the next season—as well as in the 1986–1987 and 1987–1988 seasons!

THOUGH GRETZKY HAS WON MULTIPLE STANLEY CUPS—OR NHL CHAMPIONSHIPS—THIS IS ONE RECORD HE DOESN'T HOLD. HENRI RICHARD WON 11 STANLEY CUPS BETWEEN 1956 AND 1973.

FOUR-TIME STANLEY CUP WINNER

Did You Know?

The winners of the Eastern **Conference** Finals and Western Conference Finals face each other in the Stanley Cup Finals. The team that wins the best of seven games is the winner.

Though considered one of the best NHL players today, McDavid has yet to win a Stanley Cup. In both 2024 and 2025, McDavid and the Oilers made it to the Stanley Cup Finals. Both times, they lost to the Florida Panthers.

IN 2024, MCDAVID AND THE OILERS LOST TO THE PANTHERS IN GAME SEVEN OF THE STANLEY CUP FINALS. IN 2025, THEY LOST IN GAME SIX TO THE PANTHERS.

THE HART MEMORIAL TROPHY

The NHL MVP is awarded the Hart Memorial Trophy each season. Gretzky won the honor eight years in a row—the first player to ever do that. He first won it during the 1979–1980 season during his first year playing in the NHL.

NINE HART MEMORIAL TROPHY WINS (NHL RECORD)

TWO CONN SMYTHE TROPHY WINS

GRETZKY WON THE HART TROPHY FROM THE 1979–1980 SEASON THROUGH THE 1986–1987 SEASON, AS WELL AS FOR THE 1988–1989 SEASON.

HART TROPHY

Did You Know?

Gretzky was named MVP of the Stanley Cup Finals in 1985 and 1988. The MVP of the Finals wins the Conn Smythe Trophy.

McDavid won the Hart Memorial Trophy in 2017, 2021, and 2023. In the 2022–2023 season, he led the NHL in points, goals, and assists. McDavid is only the fifth player in NHL history to lead these three stats in one season.

WILL MCDAVID BE NAMED MVP AGAIN IN HIS CAREER?

THREE HART MEMORIAL TROPHY WINS

ONE CONN SMYTHE TROPHY WIN

GIVING BACK

Both Gretzky and McDavid have shown greatness off the ice too. Gretzky founded the Wayne Gretzky Foundation in 2002. It aims to help kids from all backgrounds have a chance to play hockey.

In 2022, McDavid gave money and helped raise awareness for the Ben Stelter Foundation. It works to help children with cancer and their families, among other goals. McDavid has also taken part in other good works around Edmonton, including helping kids who are part of the **Indigenous** community.

Did You Know?

Gretzky was inducted, or put into, the Hockey Hall of Fame in 1999.

MCDAVID AND GRETZKY BOTH USE THEIR FAME TO MAKE A DIFFERENCE IN THE WORLD AROUND THEM.

GLOSSARY

competitive: Having to do with an event in which people try to beat others.

conference: A group of sports teams that compete with each other.

draft: Selecting a player from a pool of potential players entering the league. Also, the process of selecting new players.

franchise: A professional sports team that is a member of an organized league.

generation: A group of individuals born about the same time.

Indigenous: Having to do with people who are descended from early inhabitants of a place.

league: A group of sports teams that face each other.

major junior: Hockey leagues in North America for the best young players.

pandemic: A time when a disease, or sickness, spreads quickly and affects a large number of people in a place or throughout the world.

professional: Earning money from an activity that many people do for fun.

retire: To leave a job.

tournament: A series of contests testing the skill of many athletes in the same sport.

FOR MORE INFORMATION

BOOKS

Berglund, Bruce. *Hockey GOATs: The Greatest Athletes of All Time.* Mankato, MN: Capstone Press, 2024.

Lake, Theia. *20 Things You Didn't Know About Hockey.* Buffalo, NY: PowerKids Press, 2026.

WEBSITES

Connor McDavid Stats and News
www.nhl.com/oilers/player/connor-mcdavid-8478402
Keep up with McDavid on the official NHL website.

The Great One
www.gretzky.com
Find out even more about Gretzky here.

INDEX